THE GAME WITH NO RESTART

THE GAME OF ME, I AND MYSELF

GANESH YASHWANTH R

Made with ♥ on the Notion Press Platform
www.notionpress.com

To my incredible friends, family, and well-wishers—
For the unwavering support, endless encouragement, and countless memories we've shared. You have been my strength, my inspiration, and my greatest companions on this journey.

To my family, who have stood by me through every challenge and triumph—your love and belief in me have shaped who I am today.

To my friends, who have made every moment of life more vibrant and meaningful—your laughter, wisdom, and friendship have been the greatest gifts.

To my well-wishers, who have cheered for me from near and far—your kind words, guidance, and belief in my dreams have fueled my passion and determination. This book is not just mine; it carries pieces of each of you. Thank you for being part of my story.

With love and gratitude, Ganesh Yashwanth R

Contents

Preface

Life is a journey that is full of highs and lows, happy andsadtimes, and innumerable lessons learned. I've learned from my experiences that no excellent life is complete without some bad days. We develop, learn, and get stronger throughout these trying moments. I've come to the conclusion that time fixes practically everything. It's important to look forward to the future with hope and optimism since what's coming is frequently better than what's gone. I came to understand the value of resilience and flexibility as I made my way through life's many turns. All of my experiences—both positive and negative—have molded me in to the person I am now. I've come to accept the unknown with open arms and let go of things that no longer serve me. My self discovery journey has been transforming, and I hope that by sharing my story, others can find comfort and inspiration in their own journeys.

I

The Awakening Journey

I set off from Tuticorin to Chennai, my mind buzzing with thoughts of the new experiences awaiting me in college. I reached my college with my dad and his friend. I was really excited for my first day. My dad and I were busy paying my college and hostel fees. It was a busy day for both of us. After a long time, I finally paid my academic and hostel fees. My dad and I went to the college canteen and had a cup of tea. He was really proud of me for studying B.Tech Computer Science Engineering at one of the top colleges in India. We were both very happy. After completing all the processes, I finally got into the hostel. My dad left me alone, and I cried. He smiled sadly, and I couldn't forget those moments. Now I was alone and needed to take care of myself. I went into my hostel room, cleaned everything, set up my space, and called my mom to cry with her. At 5 PM, I met one of my tuition mates, Dinesh, who was also at the same college. We didn't have much conversation, and I felt really lonely. At 7 PM, I went down to the hostel mess. I liked the food and saw some Tamil-speaking people. My roommates were Telugu guys, and I didn't like that. The next day was my first day at college. I stepped in and I really liked the environment of the college. I enjoyed the moment of my first day—new place, new people. After a little struggle, I found my classroom. I met a boy named Sanjay Praveen. He was the first person I met in college, and he was really nice. We became friends. To be frank, my first day was really boring. Day one itself, maths class started. After a long day, I came back to the hostel and met Dinesh in his room, and I saw his roommates too. The two guys from Vellore, Alex and Sudharsan. They were chill and fun guys, and we became friends. I was performing well in my exams and started upskilling in cybersecurity. Days were smooth. After a few days, Alex and Sudharsan got into a fight and left each other. I stayed with Sudharsan. He taught me a lot about Chennai, and I learned much from him. Again, days went normal. In college, I met a few other guys: Vicky, Hari, and Jorisha. At that time, I didn't know these people would change my college life. I became friends with them. After a few days, I started preparing for my semester exams. I used to teach my friends too. My circle was really good compared to my school days. I did my lab activities and internals really well. Then Sudharsan and I used to fight in the hostel with some Hindi-speaking people. They broke our room door glasses and did some other unwanted activities. My semester exam was near, and I was fully focused on my studies. Finally, I completed my first semester and passed all subjects. I was really happy. My friends were also happy; they passed too. They said my teaching was good, and I was really happy for them. Some friends learned subjects from me and passed, while others saw my answer sheet in exams and passed. To be honest, I liked helping my friends. They were really good souls. I stepped into the second semester and learned all the subjects well, except French. Vicky, Sanjay, Hari, Jorisha, and I became close friends. We helped each other in many aspects. In the hostel, Sudharsan and I were close friends. The second semester was smooth. One fine day, we received news from the government about a dangerous virus spreading worldwide—COVID-19. Schools and colleges announced leave. We got 15 days off because the virus was rapidly spreading. After a few days, it became a pandemic, and we went into quarantine. The second semester was online, so I passed my second semester online. Fifteen days extended to two months, and two months extended to four months. I thought we were not going back to college anymore. Finally, I completed my first year of college.

II

Quarantine Enigma

I stepped into my second year virtually, as we were all in quarantine. Globally, the virus was spreading rapidly. My quarantine days were monotonous—9 to 5 online classes and 6 to 9 gaming sessions. My screen time increased significantly, and I often got scolded by my dad. Online classes, gaming, sleep, then repeat. These were my quarantine days. August 24 was my birthday. Everyone in my class wished me in the WhatsApp group, and some guys wished me privately. Among the wishes, one came from a number I recognized as a classmate, but I didn't know much about her. After that wish, I found myself developing a crush on her. Her name was Akshitaa Vijayakumar. She was cute and pretty like an angel. I didn't talk much with her initially, but slowly, I started to learn more about her through my friends. She was already friends with some of my friends. They were curious about why I was asking about her, but I didn't reveal my feelings to anyone. I'm not someone who believes in love at first sight. I knew that I was just attracted to her, just an infatuation. Days passed, and I completed my second year. Again, virtually, I stepped into the third year. Mrs. Deena was my class professor. I enjoyed her computer network classes and loved answering her questions. I found the subject fascinating. One day, there was an issue between Hindi students and Telugu students, and Mrs. Deena had to change the class representative. From the girls' side, she chose Akshitaa as the class representative. From the boys' side, the discussion was ongoing. All my friends voted for me as the class representative, and even Akshitaa texted me to become the class representative. I was unsure at first, but I finally accepted the role. Now, Akshitaa and I were the class representatives of the CSE-H section. Days went back to normal, and Akshitaa and I started getting to know each other. My feelings for her slowly evolved from a crush to love. I started loving her. I began listening to romantic and love songs every night. She was friendly to me, and I adored her innocent and cute character. After hiding my feelings for a long time, I finally shared them with my friend Hari. He was happy that I was in love with Akshitaa and was ready to help me. After a few days, Hari encouraged me to convey my feelings to her, but I hesitated. The fear of rejection and the uncertainty of her response weighed heavily on my mind. Finally, I gathered the courage to express my feelings. With trembling hands, I picked up my phone and called her. My heart pounded as I told her that I was in love with her and asked if she felt the same. Her response was a simple, "No." In that moment, my world shattered. I was heartbroken, and my eyes filled with tears. The pain was overwhelming, and I felt a deep sense of loss and rejection. I couldn't sleep that night, as my mind replayed the conversation over and over. I had thought she felt the same way, but I was wrong. The sadness consumed me, and I felt like I was drowning in a sea of emotions. The weight of unrequited love was unbearable, and I struggled to come to terms with the reality of the situation.

III

Echoes of Friendship

The next morning, I woke up to the sound of my phone ringing. Groggily, I reached for it, my heart pounding when I saw her name on the screen. Akshitaa was calling. She had an explanation; she said that she already had a boyfriend. I was in complete silence, not knowing what to say to her. I just apologized for what I did the previous day. I thought I had totally ruined my friendship with her. But I was wrong. She still valued our friendship a lot, and we both decided not to lose that. By the end of the conversation, we both realized that we could be good friends. After a few days, the college reopened, and the quarantine was over. I was excited to see my friends again. I decided not to stay in the hostel anymore, so I rented a house just for myself. It was not just a house; it was a place where I could find peace. I really liked that house. It saw every emotion of mine. I stepped into my third year of college, and after a long time, I saw all my friends again. I saw Akshitaa too. After that incident, we really became good friends. I helped her with academics, and she helped me too. We both started to teach each other, and as class representatives, we both enjoyed it very much. After that, I met her friend Anjali. Anjali was a really cool and bold girl. She was the one who laughed at all my jokes, and I was the one who could make her laugh easily. Me, Sanjay, Hari, Vicky, Jorisha, Akshitaa, and Anjali became good friends. We used to go out to restaurants, movies, shopping, and many more places. We laughed together, learned together, fought together, and were always together. Still, I didn't change my feelings for Akshitaa. We became really close; she was my bestie in my gang. I met other friends too, the cute couple Krithik and Harshita, who were friends with Hari and Akshitaa. My group of friends was incredibly fun and full of good vibes. My affection for Akshitaa grew deeper with each passing day. I kept my emotions hidden. One day, Anjali and Hari wanted to know whether I still had feelings for Akshitaa or not. I told them the truth, that I still had feelings for her. They both understood my emotions. Days passed, and I met the dynamic duo, Ruchita and Jayasri, who were friends with Akshitaa. I quickly became friends with them too. Whenever I talked with them, or even with Anjali, Akshitaa would get possessive. I also felt the same way when she talked to other boys. However, we never showed it to each other. At the end of the day, we would discuss our feelings. I felt like Jacob Black from the Twilight saga. I knew Akshitaa had feelings for me, but she never admitted it. However, I never asked her about it. I knew it was weird, so I just wanted to keep my feelings hidden from her. I shared my feelings and emotions only with Anjali and Hari. The next semester, we all joined an elective class, Neuro-Fuzzy and Genetic Programming. I met a girl in that class named

Shruthi. She was a brilliant girl, and we both became friends. We helped each other in academics. I also became friends with the professor of that subject, Mrs. Senthil Selvi. I was her favorite student, and she always helped me clarify my doubts in academics. I built a good bond with her. I was also Professor Deena's favorite student. I liked listening to her classes, and as a class representative, I helped her a lot as a perfect student. Professors Senthil Selvi and Deena liked me very much. They were my biggest supporters and well-wishers. Days passed, and one fine day, Anjali, Sanjay, and Vicky wanted to know what feelings Akshitaa had for me. So they planned a prank involving me. Anjali called Akshitaa and told her that she was in love with me. Vicky and I were nearby. A few minutes later, Akshitaa called me and said that Anjali was in love with me. The three of us were listening to that phone call while sitting in Anjali's house. I acted like I didn't know the matter, and Anjali and Vicky were listening to my phone call. Akshitaa said inappropriate things about Anjali because she didn't want Anjali to have a relationship with me. We three knew it was a prank. Akshitaa didn't know that. Anjali was devastated that her friend spoke poorly about her. I really felt bad for both of them. It was all because of me. I thought to fix this problem between them. They both didn't talk properly. Finally, I revealed to Akshitaa that it was a prank. That was the first and worst fight in our gang. Everyone got tense, and we ended up fighting with each other. I felt bad that day. Slowly, we all reunited, forgiving each other. One day, while surfing the internet, I came across a website called Omegle, where we could connect with anyone in the world. I connected with a girl named Vanessa from Malaysia. She was also a Tamil girl. We both became good friends online. Vanessa was a really mature and intelligent girl. We used to share our daily lives, discussing everything from our studies to our hobbies. Our conversations were always engaging and insightful. Vanessa's perspective on various topics often provided me with new insights and helped me see things differently. She was a great listener and always offered thoughtful advice. Our friendship grew stronger over time, and I valued her presence in my life. The days went by normally, with studies, outings, fun, and exams. One day, Akshitaa called me and said she had broken up with her boyfriend. I went to meet Hari and discussed this. Hari knew about her boyfriend but didn't reveal it to me. I finally made him reveal it. I talked about this with Anjali too. After a few days, they got back together. We were a little suspicious about her boyfriend, so I decided to gather information about him, and our suspicions were correct. He was texting many girls and had proposed to several on Instagram, and his communication was flirtatious too. I told Hari and Anjali, and I collected all the proof that he was a bad guy and not good with girls. He had lied about many things to Akshitaa. After I showed her the proof, her eyes were full of tears. But still, she didn't completely believe the proof. I don't know what her boyfriend did, but Akshitaa didn't believe us. That night, I got a call from Akshitaa and her boyfriend. He and I fought over the call because I had exposed his behavior and spoiled his image in front of Akshitaa. Anyway, Akshitaa didn't believe me. After a long fight with both of them, I became angry. The next day, I didn't speak with her. She was sad that I didn't speak with her. It had been one month, and I hadn't talked to her a single word. She was hurt. After one month, I really felt bad. I decided that whatever happened, I didn't want to lose my friendship with her. So, we became good friends again, and our friendship became strong after that one month.

Whatever the problem, silence is not the key to solving it. Just a few minutes of talking is enough. I didn't want to lose her friendship over a silly problem. I learned that we should forget and forgive. Ego is not bigger than our friendship. I always wanted my gang to be united as a family.

IV

Crown of Accomplishment

As I stepped into my final year of college, I couldn't believe how quickly the time had passed. My friends and I enjoyed our days to the fullest, making the most of every moment. At the same time, I focused on securing a job, so I decided to work hard and upskill my technical knowledge. Professors Deena and Senthil Selvi supported me very well. I started my own project in cybersecurity and got an internship too. All my friends began applying for jobs and upskilling themselves. During this time, my mom came to visit me in Chennai for a week. Her presence was a great source of motivation for me. She encouraged me to stay focused and work hard to secure a job. My mom also got to meet all of my friends, and we had a wonderful lunch together. It was a memorable experience, and her support meant a lot to me. One fine morning, I received an email from one of the companies scheduling a technical round for me. I was ready and gave my best in the technical round. During this job application journey, I formed a good connection and bond with some of my classmates. Akash, Dharani, Jayanand, Bhuvanesh, Karthi, and Guru were friends of my friend Sanjay, and I became friends with them too. We helped each other in this job hunt. I cracked my first technical round and received an email scheduling my second technical interview. I was really happy and attended the second round. Then, I waited for my final round email. Some of my friends who attended the second round received their emails, but I didn't, which frustrated me. My mom motivated me during this situation, reminding me to stay positive and patient. After two days, I finally got the email for my final round. I was really happy and successfully completed the final round, giving my best. I waited for my results for a few days. As I believed, I got selected by a company. My mom went back to Tuticorin, and I was sad to see her go, but I knew I had to stay focused on my goals. I shared this happy news with my mom, dad, and friends. A few of my friends also got selected by the same company. In my gang, unfortunately, Akshitaa and Sanjay were not getting any job offers. We, as friends, were there to support them, but they did not receive any emails from the companies. I felt really sad for them, but I had hope that they would soon get a job. Again, days passed well with my friends, and I started missing my college. One fine afternoon, I received another email from a different company offering a higher salary package. They scheduled me for a technical round. I attended and got selected for the next round. Soon, I received an email for the final round, which I didn't even expect. After completing the final round, I waited for my results. After a few days, I got selected by that company too. I was over the moon. Now, I had job offers from two companies. My professors congratulated me, and my parents were really proud of me. One day, Professor Deena asked me to join the college's volunteer work. I was interested and became a core committee member and event coordinator for the technical segment of a college event, a wonderful opportunity given by Professor Deena. During that event, I met a guy named Bharath. He was brilliant and laid-back. I learned many things about careers from him. Working with him was a good experience for me. I also met a few juniors: Santhosh, Anbu, and Shyam. Santhosh was calm and friendly, always with a helping mind. Anbu was bold and friendly. Shyam was intelligent and a good guy. I learned many things from them, and they became my favorite juniors in college. The event introduced me to new friends and taught me many things. It was a valuable experience for me. My involvement in the volunteer work and the event coordination did not go unnoticed. Many people in the college recognized my efforts and dedication. I received appreciation from my professors and peers, which boosted my confidence and motivated me to continue contributing to the college community. The event itself was a grand success, and I felt a sense of accomplishment seeing everything come together smoothly. It was a testament to the hard work and collaboration of everyone involved. After that, Professor Deena gave me the opportunity to conduct a webinar on ethical hacking for senior secondary school students. I eagerly accepted the challenge and began preparing for the webinar. I spent hours researching and organizing my material, ensuring that the content was both informative and engaging. On the day of the webinar, I was a bit nervous, but as I started speaking, my confidence grew. The students were attentive and asked insightful questions, which made the session interactive and enjoyable. The webinar was well-received, and I was recognized by many people in the college for my efforts. The experience of sharing my knowledge and interacting with the students was incredibly rewarding. It also helped me build my confidence in public speaking and teaching. The positive feedback I received from the students and faculty members was overwhelming, and it reinforced my belief in the importance of giving back to the community. Finally, I got a good job too. I always believed that hard work never fails and learned that the only source of knowledge is experience. The journey through my final year of college was filled with challenges, growth, and memorable experiences. The support from my professors, friends, and the new connections I made along the way played a significant role in shaping my future. As I looked back on my college years, I felt a deep sense of gratitude for all the opportunities and experiences that had come my way.

V
End of an Era

It was the last semester, and I was enjoying myself and relaxing. My school best friend, Karthikeyan, used to come to my home, and we went shopping, bike riding, and had a lot of fun together. Another school friend, Harish, also used to visit. Those were really cool and fun moments. My college friend, Akash, used to come over as well. He was preparing for the IELTS exam. His dream was to study abroad, and he cracked the IELTS after his fourth attempt. I was really impressed by his motivation for this dream. He helped me improve my lifestyle, and I learned many things about relationships and life from him. He was truly a good and hardworking soul. Days went by, but I was still in love with Akshitaa. I really liked her so much. Her friendly, innocent, and soft character made me fall for her. One day, she called me and said she had broken up with her boyfriend. She finally realized that he was not a good guy. She was crying, and I was there with her, unsure of what to do. She still hadn't gotten a job and was feeling broken. I became her emotional support. I helped her get out of her sad feelings and made her happy again. It was the last month of college life. At midnight on May 3rd, I received a call from Akshitaa. She was trying to say something but couldn't find the words. After a few minutes of talking, she finally said that she loved me. I was stunned, my heart racing as I processed her words. For a moment, I couldn't believe what I had just heard. All the emotions I had kept hidden for so long came rushing to the surface. I took a deep breath and told her that I loved her too. We talked for hours that night, sharing our feelings and dreams for the future. It felt like a weight had been lifted off my shoulders, and I was filled with a sense of happiness and relief. The next day, I went to pick her up at the bus stop, not as a friend, but as a lover. I couldn't wait to see her. That morning, we went to college together. It was a beautiful bike ride that I will never forget. She hugged me from behind, and I felt a warmth and connection that was indescribable. We spent the day together, talking and laughing like we always did, but now with a new understanding between us. Our friends noticed the change and were happy for us. It was the beginning of a new chapter in our lives, one filled with love and hope. As the final days of college approached, we made the most of every moment. I remember the day we went to the movie theater. We held hands, our hearts pounding. We could hear each other's breathing, and she leaned on my shoulder. I turned to her and gently cupped her face in my hands. She looked into my eyes, and in that moment, everything else faded away. I leaned in, and our lips met in a tender, heartfelt kiss. It was our first kiss, and it felt like magic. The world around us seemed to disappear, and all that mattered was the love we shared. As I drove back home, I couldn't stop thinking about the romance we had in the theater. It was a memory that would stay with me forever. I used to visit her house, and we shared some romantic moments. We didn't just connect physically; we touched each other's souls. Our time together was filled with deep conversations and heartfelt moments. It was a love that transcended the physical and touched the very core of our beings. One day, she surprised me with a gift—a T-shirt. It was a simple gesture, but it meant the world to me. Every time I wore it, I felt her presence and the love she had for me. Days passed, and college life came to an end. My friends and I planned a trip to the mall and an aquarium by car. We had a lot of fun and enjoyed every moment. As we drove to the mall, we sang along to our favorite songs, reminiscing about our college days. At the mall, we shopped for souvenirs and took countless photos to capture the memories. The aquarium was the highlight of our trip. We marveled at the colorful marine life, watched the mesmerizing movements of the fish, and even touched some of the sea creatures in the interactive exhibits. It was a day filled with joy and camaraderie, a perfect way to celebrate the end of an era. As the sun set, we gathered for a final meal together, sharing stories and making promises to stay in touch. It was a bittersweet moment, knowing that our college days were behind us, but also feeling excited about the future. We knew that no matter where life took us, the bond we shared would remain strong. Afterward, Akshitaa and I cried together, overwhelmed by the emotions of the day.While riding the bike, she wrapped her arms around me from behind, her embrace warm and tender. She playfully bit my shoulder, sending a shiver down my spine. I then dropped her off at her home, cherishing the time we had spent together and the memories we had created. The ride back was filled with a sense of romance and connection that lingered in the air, a beautiful memory etched in my heart.

After I got back home, I called her, and we talked for a long time. The next day, I was about to leave Chennai, so she came to my home in the morning to help me pack my things. As we packed, we reminisced about our time together and shared our hopes for the future. It was a bittersweet moment, knowing that we would be apart for a while, but also feeling grateful for the bond we had built. She helped me organize my belongings, and we made sure everything was ready for my departure. In the midst of packing, we shared a tender moment. She sat down, and I gently applied nail polish to her nails. It was a simple act, but it felt intimate and special. We laughed and talked, savoring the time we had left together. It was a beautiful memory that I would cherish forever. Afterward, we ordered lunch and she fed me, a gesture that felt both loving and playful. We both enjoyed ice cream, sharing bites and laughing at each other's messy faces. As we finished packing, we found ourselves standing close, our eyes locked. Slowly, we leaned in and shared a series of soft, heartfelt kisses. Each kiss felt like a promise, a testament to the love we shared. The sensation of her lips on mine was electrifying, sending waves of warmth and affection through my entire being. It was a moment of pure connection, and I knew I would carry it with me always. When it was time to leave, we hugged tightly, not wanting to let go. I promised her that we would stay in touch and visit each other whenever possible. Finally, we arrived at the railway station, and we both cried. As we stood there, holding each other tightly, the reality of our separation hit us hard. The tears flowed freely, and we didn't care about the people around us. It was a moment of raw emotion, a testament to the deep bond we shared. As the train approached, we shared one last kiss, filled with love and longing. I boarded the train, and she waved goodbye, her eyes filled with tears. As the train pulled away, I couldn't help but feel a mix of sadness and hope. I knew that our love would endure, and that this was just the beginning of a new chapter in our lives. The beautiful moments spent with friends and loved ones are priceless. It's essential to cherish these moments and create lasting memories. Love and friendship are the cornerstones of a fulfilling life, and it's the little things that often make the biggest difference.

VI

Separated by Miles, United by Love

My college life came to an end, filled with fun, fights, drama, and everything in between. I returned to Tuticorin, and I missed Akshitaa so much. We couldn't meet in person, but we chatted daily. As the days went by, our conversations became the highlight of my day. We shared our experiences, dreams, and challenges, supporting each other from afar. Despite the distance, our bond grew stronger, and I felt grateful for the connection we had. One day, she surprised me with a video call. Seeing her face and hearing her voice made me realize how much I cherished our relationship. We talked for hours, laughing and reminiscing about our college days. It was a beautiful reminder of the love we shared and the memories we had created. After a few days, we received an email from the college to collect our provisional certificates. I was excited to see her again. I booked a train ticket and went to Chennai to collect my certificates. I stayed at the junior boys' home with

Santhosh, Anbu, and Shyam. It was wonderful to see my favorite juniors again and catch up with them. Santhosh even gave me his bike and helped me. I saw her in the college canteen, waiting for me. We were both happy to see each other. We went to collect the certificates from Professor Deena and told her about our love. She was happy for us. After collecting our certificates, we decided to spend the day together. We visited our favorite spots on campus, reminiscing about the memories we had created during our college days. We laughed, took photos, and enjoyed each other's company. It felt like we were reliving those precious moments all over again. We went to see a movie, and during the film, we shared some romantic moments and kisses. It felt magical to be so close to her again. After the movie, we had lunch together and then visited a nearby temple to pray and seek blessings for our future. As the day came to an end, we sat down for a quiet moment, reflecting on our journey and the love we shared. Finally, we reached the metro train station, and tears began to flow. As we embraced tightly, the reality of our impending separation struck us deeply. I left her at the metro train station, my heart heavy with sadness. As I rode my bike back home, tears streamed down my face. The pain of leaving her was overwhelming, and I couldn't stop crying. It was a moment of profound sadness, but also a testament to the depth of our love. I returned to Tuticorin once again. The days were filled with constant texting and video calls. After a few days, we had our graduation ceremony at college. We met each other again with full excitement and joy. We also reunited with our friends, sharing laughter and memories. The graduation ceremony was a beautiful event, marking the end of an important chapter in our lives. We took photos, exchanged hugs, and celebrated our achievements together. It was a day filled with pride and happiness, knowing that we had accomplished so much. After that, on August 24th, my birthday, she sent me a courier. It was a gift for me—a shirt and a silver bracelet. Receiving her thoughtful gift made my day even more special. I felt her love and care through the presents, and it brought a smile to my face. We continued to stay connected through texts and video calls, sharing our daily lives and supporting each other from afar. As time went on, we both focused on our careers and personal growth. I helped her find a job, and she successfully got hired. However, her mom didn't allow her to take the job due to the low salary. Despite this setback, we continued to support each other. I encouraged her to keep looking for better opportunities and assured her that something suitable would come along. We spent hours discussing her career goals and exploring different options. On October 6th, her birthday, I told my mom that I was going to attend an interview with another company, but in reality, I went to see her. The excitement of seeing her again was overwhelming. I arrived at her place with a small gift, hoping to make her day special. When she saw me, her face lit up with joy. We spent the day together, celebrating her birthday and creating new memories. We laughed, talked, and enjoyed each other's company, cherishing every moment we had. We went to a restaurant for a special birthday lunch. The atmosphere was perfect, and we shared a delicious meal while reminiscing about our time together. It was a beautiful and intimate moment, filled with love and happiness. Despite the pressure from our parents and the challenges we faced, our love remained strong. We knew that we had to be careful and discreet, but we were determined to make our relationship work. The time we spent together on her birthday was a reminder of the deep bond we shared and the love that kept us going. As the day came to an end, we promised each other that we would continue to fight for our love, no matter what obstacles came our way. Our love was a constant source of strength and comfort. Despite the challenges and pressures from our families, our love remained unwavering. It was a testament to the deep bond we shared and the commitment we had to each other. The moments we spent together, whether it was a simple conversation or a special celebration, created lasting memories that we would cherish forever.

VII
Emotional Maze

Our long-distance relationship continued, but the situation became more complicated when our parents found out about our love. The problem was serious, as both of our parents did not accept our relationship. The pressure from our families was immense, and they constantly reminded us of their disapproval. They tried to convince us to end our relationship, making it difficult for us to stay connected. Her parents asked Akshitaa to either marry someone or go abroad for higher studies. They didn't respect me because I came from a middle-class family with a low status. Akshitaa decided not to marry anyone, so she accepted the option of pursuing higher studies abroad. Her parents believed that I couldn't afford to study abroad, which meant I wouldn't be able to meet her anymore. They planned for her to study in Germany. Akshitaa asked me to come to Germany for higher studies so that she could convince her parents. However, I wasn't in a position to plan for higher studies abroad because I had just received a job offer. It was the result of my hard work, and I didn't want to let it go. This led to a significant fight between us. The argument was intense and emotional. She felt that I wasn't prioritizing our relationship, while I believed that I needed to secure my future first. We both said things we didn't mean, and the fight left us both feeling hurt and misunderstood. The pressure from our parents and the uncertainty of our future together weighed heavily on us. Despite the fight, we knew that our love was strong. We decided to take some time to cool off and reflect on our situation. It was a difficult period, but we hoped that we could find a way to make things work. Due to the fight between us, we didn't talk much. Our communication dwindled, and her parents didn't even allow me to connect with her. Even though we used to talk late at night, it often ended in arguments. The love and longing we felt turned into countless apologies and pleas for forgiveness. We both cried a lot, overwhelmed by the confusion between our future and our love, which led to even more fights. For many days, I anxiously awaited my job's date of joining letter, but no email arrived. I felt frustrated and lost, like I was in the dark. I didn't know what to do. Akshitaa wasn't talking to me, and I felt incredibly lonely. There was no one to understand my feelings. During this difficult time, I decided to go abroad to Germany. At least, I could secure my love. So, I asked my parents for their suggestion, but I didn't tell them that Akshitaa was also going to Germany. I knew they wouldn't allow me to go if they knew the real reason. I hid that from my parents. They still asked me to wait for the date of joining from the company. However, I managed to convince them and made them accept my decision to pursue higher studies in Germany. True love can inspire us to overcome even the most challenging obstacles. Our determination to be together, despite the disapproval of our families, showed me the strength of our bond.

VIII
Quest for Love and Knowledge

I took a week to plan my higher studies process and researched more about it. I selected the universities and decided to pursue an MSc in Cybersecurity. I started with the IELTS exam, an English proficiency test for those who want to study abroad. It felt like a golden ticket for me, and I began preparing hard for the exam with full motivation. This was for both my love and my career. As I delved deeper into the preparation, I realized the magnitude of the challenge ahead. However, the thought of being with Akshitaa and building a future together kept me motivated. I knew that this was a chance to not only secure my love but also to advance my career and personal growth. I reached out to my friend Akash about the process and the IELTS exam. He helped me a lot, as he was also in the process of going to London for his higher studies. He sent me study materials and motivated me immensely. I finally applied for the exam, gave it my best, and completed it. I waited anxiously for 15 days for the results to arrive. Early one morning at 5 AM, the results came in. Sadly, I didn't get the score I needed. I told Akshitaa about it, but she didn't seem to care. She was still angry with me and busy with her own process of going abroad. I shared the news with my mom, and she became really sad. I felt lost and didn't know what to do. I asked my mom for money to retake the exam, which cost 17,000 rupees. She gave it to me from her savings, her eyes full of hope that I would pass the next time. Determined to succeed, I decided to focus entirely on my preparation for the next month. With renewed determination, I immersed myself in my studies. I followed a strict schedule, dedicating hours each day to practice and review. Akash continued to support me, providing valuable tips and encouragement. His belief in my abilities kept me motivated. One day, Akshitaa texted me that she had received her visa for Germany. I was happy for her that she made it, but she was still angry with me, and I didn't know the reason for her anger. Even though I was doing all this for her, I suspected that her parents might have influenced her. Despite my overthinking, I balanced my studies for the exam to give my best next time. I really wanted to talk to her because it had been a long time since we had spoken. So, I decided to call her, and she picked up the phone. I asked about the status of her plans for going to Germany. She replied that she had already arrived in Germany a week ago. My heart felt heavy knowing that she didn't even tell me she was going. I didn't know what was happening. I thought she might have slowly lost interest in me, but I didn't give up on my love. As the exam date approached, I felt more confident and prepared. I knew that this was my chance to prove myself and secure my future with Akshitaa. On the day of the exam, I gave it my all, leaving no stone unturned. After completing the exam, I felt a sense of relief and accomplishment. I knew I had done my best, and now it was time to wait for the results once again. The anticipation was nerve-wracking, but I remained hopeful. Finally, the day arrived when the results were released. With bated breath, I checked my score. This time, I had achieved the score I needed. Overwhelmed with joy, I shared the news with my mom, who was equally ecstatic. Her faith in me had paid off. I also informed Akshitaa, hoping that this would bring us closer together. Despite the challenges we faced, I was determined to make our relationship work and build a future together. I started the next step to get the LOR certificate from my professors. It's an important document for my higher education abroad. I went to Chennai again and stayed at my juniors' house. I told them that I was going to Germany, and they were happy for me. I went to college to get the LOR certificate from my professors, who were genuinely pleased for me. As I walked through the college campus, memories of my time with Akshitaa flooded back. I remembered the countless hours we spent together, studying in the classroom, sharing meals in the canteen, and laughing with friends. Every corner of the campus held a special memory of our love and the moments we cherished. I visited the spots where we used to hang out, reminiscing about the times we shared. These memories brought a smile to my face and a sense of nostalgia. Collecting the LOR certificate from my professors was a significant step towards my future, but it also reminded me of the beautiful past I had with Akshitaa. Despite the challenges we faced, these memories gave me the strength to keep moving forward and pursue my dreams. While coming back to Tuticorin, I cried on the bus, remembering my past days with my friends and the romantic times with

Akshitaa. The memories of our time together flooded my mind, and the weight of our current situation felt overwhelming. I missed the carefree days we spent laughing and enjoying each other's company. The thought of not being able to share those moments again brought tears to my eyes. As I sat on the bus, I reflected on the journey ahead. I knew that pursuing higher studies in Germany was a significant step, not just for my career but also for my relationship with Akshitaa. Despite the challenges and uncertainties, I was determined to make it work. For the next step, I needed to pay the fee for my shortlisted university, but I didn't have enough cash for that. So, I decided to get a job in my city. For a long time, Akshitaa didn't talk to me. When I called her, she didn't show any interest in me. Despite the distance and her lack of interest, I continued to help her with her studies and academics. I created resumes for her and applied for part-time jobs on her behalf. Simultaneously, I searched for a job for myself. Balancing my job and preparing for my higher studies was challenging, but I remained focused on my goal. I knew that securing a job would help me save money for my university fees and bring me one step closer to being with Akshitaa. Even in the face of adversity, holding onto hope and persevering through difficult times can lead to positive outcomes. No matter how dark it gets, I learned to never give up on myself.

IX
Resurgence of Willpower

After a few days, I got a job as a computer programming staff member at an institute in my city. Balancing my new job and preparing for my higher studies was challenging, but I remained focused on my goal. The first day at the institute was really boring for me. The institute admin, Amutha, introduced me to all the other staff members. All the other staff members were women, and they were older than me. I felt uncomfortable and isolated because no one considered me. However, I was wrong. The next day, a staff member named Kanimozhi spoke with me. She was really kind and friendly, and she was the first person to talk to me. After that, I felt less isolated. On the third day, another staff member named Raji spoke with me. Initially, I thought she was a serious type, but she turned out to be fun and friendly. From that day on, other staff members started talking to me as well. Even the admin, Amutha, became friends with me. Sometimes, I would sit in a class to learn other programming languages. A staff member named Archana taught very well. Slowly, I became friends with everyone, especially Kanimozhi and Raji, who became really close to me. The three of us would go to the tea shop in the evening and talk about our lives. They shared their problems and happiness with me. The workplace became a pleasant environment for me. Every morning, I looked forward to coming to the office just to chat with them. I enjoyed being part of their circle. As time went on, I felt more comfortable and integrated into the team. I also took the opportunity to learn new programming languages by sitting in on classes. Archana, one of the staff members, was an excellent teacher, and I gained valuable knowledge from her lessons. My job at the institute not only helped me save money for my university fees but also provided me with a supportive and friendly environment. The camaraderie with my colleagues made the workdays enjoyable and less stressful. Despite the positive atmosphere at work, I couldn't shake off the thoughts of Akshitaa and our strained relationship. I continued to focus on my studies and preparations for higher education, hoping that one day we would be able to overcome the challenges and be together. But I was wrong. On July 2nd, she broke up with me. I felt utterly devastated and cried uncontrollably. I didn't expect this from her, and the pain was overwhelming. The heartbreak was like a heavy weight on my chest, making it hard to breathe. I couldn't understand why she had decided to end things, especially after all the efforts I had put in to make our relationship work. The memories of our time together haunted me, and I felt a deep sense of loss and betrayal. Every moment we had shared, every laugh, every tear, every promise we made to each other seemed to crumble before my eyes. The future I had envisioned with her now felt like a distant dream, shattered into pieces. The emotional turmoil was unbearable, and I felt like I was drowning in sorrow. Despite the heartbreak, I knew I had to keep moving forward. I continued to focus on my job and my preparations for higher studies. The support from my colleagues at the institute helped me cope with the emotional turmoil. Kanimozhi and Raji, in particular, were there for me, offering a listening ear and words of encouragement. After a few days, I started teaching my first class. Some of my students became friends with me. One day, my students Sathish and Vedha planned a tour to Kanyakumari. All the staff and students went on the tour. The trip to Kanyakumari was a refreshing break from our routine. We visited the famous landmarks and attractions there, enjoying the scenic beauty and the serene atmosphere. The students were excited, and their enthusiasm was contagious. We took a lot of photos, capturing the memories of our time together. During the tour, I got to know my students and colleagues better. Kanimozhi and Raji enjoyed the trip very much, and our friendship grew stronger. We shared stories, laughed, and bonded over the experiences. The trip helped strengthen our relationships and created a sense of camaraderie among us. While coming back from Kanyakumari, Kanimozhi was there to be an emotional support. We sat nearby, enjoying each other's company and sharing our thoughts and feelings. As we returned from the tour, I felt a renewed sense of purpose and motivation. The support and friendship of my students and colleagues made me feel more confident and determined to achieve my goals. I continued to focus on my job and my preparations for higher studies, knowing that I had a strong support system behind me. Life is full of unexpected changes and challenges. Adapting to new environments and situations, like my job at the institute, helped me grow and become more resilient. Despite the emotional turmoil of my breakup, I remained focused on my goals. Persevering through tough times and staying committed to my aspirations allowed me to make progress and move forward. Heartbreak and disappointment are inevitable parts of life. Learning to process and overcome these emotions is crucial for personal growth and well-being.

X
Rebirth of Self

After a few weeks, I received a date of joining email from the company where I had been selected earlier. So, I needed to leave the city and move to Chennai again. Leaving my job at the institute and saying goodbye to my colleagues was bittersweet. I had formed strong bonds with Kanimozhi, Raji, and the other staff members, and it was hard to leave them behind. Kanimozhi and Raji, in particular, were visibly saddened by my departure. They had become close friends, and the thought of not seeing each other every day was difficult for all of us. Kanimozhi expressed her sadness, saying how much she would miss our evening tea shop conversations and the support we provided each other. Raji, who had always been fun and friendly, shared her feelings of loss and how much she valued our friendship. Their heartfelt words made the farewell even more emotional. However, I knew that this new opportunity was a significant step towards achieving my goals. As I prepared to move to Chennai, I felt a mix of excitement and nervousness. The thought of starting a new job and the possibilities it held for my future kept me motivated. I packed my belongings and bid farewell to my friends and family, ready to embark on this new journey. All my institute friends came to see me off at the railway station. Their presence made the farewell even more emotional. Kanimozhi and Raji, in particular, were visibly saddened by my departure. They had become close friends, and the thought of not seeing each other every day was difficult for all of us. We shared heartfelt goodbyes, and they wished me the best for my new journey. As the train started moving, I waved goodbye to my friends, feeling a mix of sadness and excitement. Leaving behind the familiar faces and the supportive environment of the institute was tough, but I knew that this new opportunity in Chennai was a significant step towards achieving my goals. My school friend Harish was already working in Chennai, so he helped me find accommodation. I settled in, and the next day was my first day at the company. I had waited a long time for this opportunity, and I was excited. The first day at the company was filled with anticipation and nervousness. The office was bustling with activity, and I felt a sense of excitement in the air. Training started for me. The company and the training were good, but the people in my training group were boring and didn't match my vibe. After a few days, Kanimozhi got a government job in Chennai, and she really took care of me. We both helped each other in many aspects, and I was happy to have one of my institute friends nearby. We used to go out, do shopping, and engage in various activities in Chennai. Days went by peacefully. Having Kanimozhi around made the transition to my new job much smoother. Her presence provided a sense of familiarity and comfort in the bustling city. We explored different parts of Chennai together, discovering new places to eat, shop, and relax. Our friendship grew stronger as we shared our experiences and supported each other through the challenges of our new jobs. The initial boredom of the training group faded as I focused on my work and built new connections. Ruban and Sibi were both in the same accommodation and training group as me. Ruban's hometown was near mine, so we quickly became close. My vibe matched well with both Ruban and Sibi. We helped each other during training and completed tasks and exams together. Having Ruban and Sibi around made the training period more enjoyable and less stressful. We formed a strong bond and supported each other through the challenges. Our teamwork and camaraderie helped us excel in our training. As the days went by, we continued to strengthen our friendship. We spent time together outside of work, exploring the city and enjoying various activities. With the training completed, we were ready to take on new responsibilities at the company. The skills and knowledge we gained during the training period prepared us well for the challenges ahead. Ruban and I became really close through playing games together. He was exceptionally good at gaming. During our gaming sessions, he would share stories about his life, and I would share mine. After a few days, I decided to call Akshitaa. She had blocked me on everything, so I called her using Ruban's phone. I spoke with her to see if she still had feelings for me, but she didn't. That was my last call to her, and I decided to move on from her. Ruban and Kanimozhi helped me get through this difficult time. They both motivated me and provided the support I needed. Ruban would teach me life lessons whenever we went to the tea shop. Playing games and going to the tea shop with him helped relieve my stress and made me feel better. Ruban was truly a good soul. As I continued to settle into my new job and life in Chennai, I found solace in the friendships I had built. I decided to let go of my dream of studying in Germany, understanding my parents' financial situation and realizing that, as I was now earning, I should take care of them. This decision was not easy, but it felt like the right thing to do. My parents had always supported me, and it was time for me to give back. I focused on my job and continued to work hard, knowing that my efforts were helping to support my family. Ruban, in particular, was a great source of wisdom and motivation. He taught me valuable life lessons during our tea shop visits, and our gaming sessions provided much-needed stress relief. My institute friend Raji used to call me whenever possible. I knew she missed me, and I missed those moments with them too. Soon, my place at the institute was replaced by a girl named Harithaa. She became friends with Raji and took care of her on my behalf. Through Raji, I was introduced to Harithaa. We connected on social media and became good friends. Having Harithaa in Raji's life gave me some comfort, knowing that Raji had someone to rely on. Our friendship with Harithaa grew stronger over time, and we often chatted and shared our experiences. It felt good to have a new friend who understood the bond I shared with Raji. As I continued to settle into my life in Chennai, I found a balance between work and personal life. I realized that life is full of unexpected connections and that each new friendship brings its own unique joy and support. I focused on my career and personal growth. I continued to learn new skills and take on new responsibilities at the company. The challenges I faced only fueled my determination to succeed. From my life journey, I've learned many things. A good life needs some bad days, and I've come to understand that time heals almost everything. What's coming is better than

what's gone. I've realized that everything is temporary –
thoughts, feelings, people, and even places. I've decided to
free my mind and just go with the flow. In the end, I've come
to know that I'm going to end up with Me, I and Myself.